WORKBOOK FOR
RADICAL ACCEPTANCE

Embracing Your Life With the Heart of a Buddha: A Practical Guide For Implementing Tara Brach's Book

DAVIS READS

Disclaimer!!!

This book is a companion book designed for informational and educational purposes only. The content is based on the ideas presented in the main book but it is not endorsed or affiliated with the author or publisher of the main book.

The workbook is intended to complement and enhance the main book, offering readers additional tools for personal growth and self-reflection. However, the workbook should not be considered a substitute for professional advice, diagnosis, or treatment.

While every effort has been made to ensure the accuracy and completeness of the information in this workbook, the publisher and author assume no responsibility for errors, inaccuracies, or omissions.

This book belongs to

_____

_____

_____

Table Of Contents

How To Use This Book.. 5

Overview Of The Main Book.. 7

Chapter One: Looking for a Better Way..................... 9

    Key Lessons... 9

    Self Reflection Questions..11

Chapter Two: The "Answers"..................................... 15

    Key Lessons... 15

    Self Reflection Questions...................................... 17

Chapter Three: Creating Positive Change That Lasts. 21

    Key Lessons... 21

    Self Reflection Questions...................................... 23

Chapter Four: New Discoveries............................... 28

    Key Lessons... 28

    Self Reflection Questions...................................... 31

Chapter 5: We Learn to Believe................................36

    Key Lessons... 36

    Self Reflection Questions...................................... 38

Chapter Six: The Wall..43

    Key Lessons... 43

    Self Reflection Questions...................................... 45

Chapter Seven: Passing It On................................... 50

    Key Lessons... 50

    Self Reflection Questions...................................... 52

Chapter 8: The Self-Management Sequence............57

Key Lessons.. 57

Self Reflection Questions................................. 59

Chapter Nine: The Five Levels of Self-Talk.............. 65

Key Lessons.. 65

Self Reflection Questions................................. 69

Chapter Ten: A New Look at Positive Thinking....... 74

Key Lessons.. 74

Self Reflection Questions................................. 77

Final Evaluation Questions.......................................81

Note...89

How To Use This Book

Prepare Your Space: Find a place that is quiet and comfortable where you can work on the workbook after receiving it. Creating a serene environment will help you focus and engage with the material effectively.

Review the Instructions: Before you begin, take a moment to read and understand the instructions and prompts provided in each section of the workbook. Clear comprehension of the requirements will facilitate a more meaningful exploration of the book's concepts.

Writing Tools: You'll need a pen or pencil to complete the workbook. Ensure you have these writing tools readily available before you start, along with any additional materials like notebooks or paper.

Manage Your Energy: To prevent eye strain or bodily discomfort, it's advisable to take breaks as needed while working through the workbook. Stretch, relax, and return to the exercises with a refreshed mind.

Seek Guidance: If you encounter any questions or concerns during your workbook journey, don't hesitate to contact a professional, therapist, or counselor. They can provide guidance and support as you delve into self-reflection and personal growth.

Reflect and Apply: Upon completing the workbook, take time to reflect on what you've learned and how you can integrate these insights into your daily life. Consider the practical applications of the concepts explored in "Radical Acceptance" by Tara Brach and how they can contribute to your well-being and relationships.

Remember that this workbook is a valuable companion to your reading of the book. It is designed to help you engage more deeply with the content, fostering self-awareness, personal growth, and the practical application of radical acceptance principles in your life. Enjoy your journey of exploration and transformation.

Overview Of The Main Book

Radical Acceptance is a book that highlights the necessity of accepting our flaws and embracing our common core. It enables us to react to our reality with full wisdom and compassion, enabling us to confront and respond to the pain caused by racism, unfairness, and privilege. Many students and readers have spiritually awakened as a result of radical acceptance methods after confronting hardships such as parenthood, divorce, job loss, addictive habits, and significant sickness or conflicts.

In today's society, we are experiencing a collective spiritual crisis as we lose sight of our connection to one another and to the living land. This separation necessitates the medication of radical acceptance, a clear and openhearted presence that reconnects us with life. Radical acceptance enables us to love ourselves and one another toward healing and spiritual awakening.

Tibetan Buddhism depicts the universal forces of fear, wrath, greed, and illusion through mandalas and temples to demonstrate how this enlightenment happens. We may awaken to these primordial energies and convert ourselves into a loving presence by connecting with these shadow deities with a conscious presence. We may truly embody and become that awake, loving presence, home in a holy place by providing our persistent and gentle presence.

The author describes how extreme acceptance may alter the shadow deities. They recollect a recent episode in Washington, D.C., in which they felt the wrath and blame for the insurgency, leading to anxiety and despair. However, when they allowed themselves to attention to the growing feelings, they saw that the despair was imbedded in compassion and sadness. This insight caused a change in perspective, enabling them to react with clarity and kindness rather than wrath.

When confronted with fear-based emotions like wrath and blame, the author highlights the significance of practicing radical acceptance. This helps people to perceive others' human frailty and common humanity, resulting in healing and a more compassionate society. The author also emphasizes the significance of having a "Strong Back" and a "Soft Front" in life, which involves clarity, limits, bravery, empowerment, and the desire to protect ourselves and others from harm.

Evolutionary psychologists think that human-to-human aggression has decreased through time, but this does not necessarily imply that our species is entering a dark age. It is critical that we devote ourselves to confronting and changing the shadow deities of fear and hate that separate us. We may sow seeds of real healing and progress from separation to connection through training our hearts and awareness, as well as practicing radical acceptance with one another. This may be done in a variety of circumstances, such as face-to-face conversations or observations about someone we may or may not know.

Tara Brach's Radical Acceptance is a transforming guide that examines the way of accepting one's existence with a loving heart, pulling inspiration from Buddhist teachings and mindfulness techniques. The book delves into the deep path of self-acceptance and provides practical techniques for navigating the problems of self-doubt, judgment, and inner conflict. The notion of "Radical Acceptance" entails the practice of non-judgmental, aware, and compassionate presence, which is vital in resolving self-perceived faults, accepting age, mourning the death of loved ones, and tackling social concerns such as racism, injustice, and division.

Brach stresses the necessity of noticing and treating both inner and outside conflicts, since projecting negativity onto others and ourselves creates suffering and separation. Individuals may break out from the cycle of animosity by fostering radical acceptance. The book also highlights the significance of compassion in radical acceptance, citing Civil Rights pioneer Ruby Sales, who asks, "Where does it hurt?" This inquiry encourages people to see beyond destructive actions and understand the underlying pain and suffering that motivates them.

Brach also highlights the need to have a "Strong Back and a Soft Front," which blends clarity, bravery, and limits with acceptance, kindness, and caring while managing life's obstacles. Finally, "Radical Acceptance" provides readers with a thorough investigation of self-compassion and mindfulness as a way of healing and change, making it a great resource for individuals seeking personal development and spiritual awakening.

Chapter One: The Trance of Unworthiness

Key Lessons

Tara Brach exposes readers to the widespread and crippling sense of feeling unworthy in this first chapter. She investigates how this feeling of unworthiness, dubbed "the trance," underpins most of people's suffering. Here are the important takeaways from Chapter One:

The Trance of Unworthiness: Brach defines the "trance of unworthiness" as a state of mind in which people continually assess and condemn themselves. This self-judgment leads to a deep and painful sense of not being good enough, loving enough, or worthy of pleasure.

The roots of Unworthiness: Brach digs into the roots of unworthiness, stating that it generally arises from childhood experiences, cultural training, and social pressures. These forces foster a mental habit of self-doubt and self-criticism.

The Effects of Unworthiness: This chapter discusses how unworthiness may influence every part of a person's life, influencing relationships, jobs, and general well-being. It may cause feelings of loneliness, anxiety, melancholy, and a sensation of being separated from one's genuine self.

Escaping the Trance: Brach highlights the necessity of identifying the trance of unworthiness and the misery it produces. She invites readers to break away from this trance by practicing mindfulness and self-compassion.

The Role of Mindfulness: Mindfulness, the practice of being present in the moment without judgment, is offered as a valuable tool for breaking the trance. Brach says that by being aware of our thoughts and feelings without harsh self-judgment, we may begin to heal and improve our connection with ourselves.

The Invitation to Radical Acceptance: Chapter One serves as an invitation to engage on the road of radical acceptance. According to Brach, the first step toward self-compassion and healing is to acknowledge our unworthiness without judgment.

Practice: Brach advises readers to begin practicing mindfulness by simply noticing their thoughts and emotions, especially those connected to feelings of unworthiness. Individuals may begin to emerge from the trance by doing so, revealing a more compassionate and honest self.

Self Reflection Questions

How has the trance of unworthiness materialized in your life, influencing your ideas, actions, and emotions?

_____

_____

_____

_____

_____

_____

_____

Consider the sources of your own feeling of unworthiness. To what degree do childhood events, social forces, or cultural conditioning contribute to this belief?

_____

_____

_____

_____

_____

_____

_____

In what ways has your sense of unworthiness influenced your interactions with others? Consider both personal and professional ties.

_____

_____

_____

_____

_____

_____

_____

_____

Can you pinpoint certain thinking patterns or self-critical voices that contribute to your sense of unworthiness? How do they appear in your inner dialogue?

_____

_____

_____

_____

_____

_____

_____

_____

What methods or coping mechanisms have you employed to avoid or dull the ache of feeling unworthy? Are these techniques beneficial or damaging in the long run?

_____

_____

_____

_____

_____

_____

_____

_____

How do you presently practice mindfulness in your life, if at all? Consider times when mindfulness helped you to break away from the hypnosis of unworthiness and reconnect with your genuine self.

_____

_____

_____

_____

_____

_____

Consider a life in which you truly embrace radical acceptance and self-compassion, free of the thrall of unworthiness. What changes do you anticipate to see in your relationships, your career, and your general well-being?

_____

_____

_____

_____

_____

_____

_____

Chapter Two: Awakening from the Trance: The Path of Radical Acceptance

Key Lessons

Recognizing the Trance: This chapter continues to look at the "trance" of unworthiness and how it affects your life. It underlines the necessity of identifying when you are trapped in this trance as the first step toward change.

The Radical Acceptance Road: Tara Brach proposes the notion of "Radical Acceptance" as a road to release from suffering. It entails accepting your experiences and feelings without judgment, which leads to self-compassion and healing.

The Power of Mindfulness: Mindfulness is emphasized as a critical tool for rising from trance. You may break away from the hold of self-judgment by practicing awareness.

Brach explains the fortitude required to confront your inner demons, as well as the vulnerability that occurs when you accept your grief. She thinks that accepting vulnerability is a way to authenticity.

Resistance to your emotions and experiences is discussed as a frequent response when confronted with discomfort. The chapter emphasizes that opposing your reality simply prolongs your suffering and that accepting it with extreme acceptance is the path ahead.

Self Reflection Questions

Have you been able to detect when you are trapped in the spell of unworthiness? What are the most prevalent indicators or triggers for you?

_____

_____

_____

_____

_____

_____

_____

_____

Consider a recent situation in which you fought or criticized your own feelings or circumstances. How did this resistance affect your well-being and inner peace?

_____

_____

_____

_____

_____

_____

_____

What does "Radical Acceptance" mean to you? How comfortable are you with the notion of embracing all of your experiences and feelings, especially the unpleasant ones, without judgment?

_____

_____

_____

_____

_____

_____

_____

Consider a period when you practiced mindfulness. How did this exercise help you become more aware of your thoughts and emotions? Did it bring any respite from the thrall of unworthiness?

_____

_____

_____

_____

_____

Consider the vulnerability notion described in the chapter. Can you think of a time when you embraced vulnerability and honesty in your life? How did it affect your relationships and self-acceptance?

_____

_____

_____

_____

_____

_____

_____

Consider your usual reaction to physical or emotional suffering. Do you prefer to reject these sensations, divert yourself, or numb them in any way? How could your experience differ if you addressed discomfort with radical acceptance?

_____

_____

_____

_____

_____

_____

_____

Consider a life in which you continuously travel the road of extreme acceptance. How do you see your connection with yourself and others changing as a result?

_____

_____

_____

_____

_____

_____

Chapter Three: The Sacred Pause: Resting Under the Bodhi Tree

Key Lessons

The Need for Pausing: Tara Brach explains the notion of the "sacred pause," highlighting the need to take periods of calm and thought in your everyday life. This pause helps you to go from instinctive reflexes to conscious awareness.

The chapter addresses how habitual responses to stress and discomfort keep you imprisoned in a trance of unworthiness. You may break out of this loop by stopping and being more conscious.

The Bodhi Tree as a Symbol: The Bodhi tree, beneath which the Buddha obtained enlightenment, serves as a symbol of awakening in this chapter. Brach advises you to seek for your own "Bodhi tree," a haven of inner sanctuary and understanding.

Embracing Stillness and Silence: Silence and stillness are portrayed as partners on your road to waking. Brach teaches you how to nurture these traits in your life, enabling you to connect with your genuine self.

Practicing the holy Pause: This chapter provides practical exercises and meditation methods to help you integrate the holy pause into your everyday practice. These activities help you react to life's obstacles with more awareness and compassion.

Self Reflection Questions

How frequently do you stop and be still in your regular life? Consider the influence of these pauses on your general well-being and alertness.

_____

_____

_____

_____

_____

_____

_____

Consider a recent instance in which you responded immediately to stress or pain. What feelings or ideas triggered your reaction, and how may a holy pause have changed your response?

_____

_____

_____

_____

_____

_____

_____

_____

The Bodhi tree represents enlightenment. What is your own "Bodhi tree," a location or practice that allows you to connect with your inner knowledge and insight?

_____

_____

_____

_____

_____

_____

_____

How at ease are you with quiet and stillness? Do
you find it difficult to accept these aspects in your
life, or do you welcome them as chances for
self-reflection?

_____

_____

_____

_____

_____

_____

_____

_____

Investigate the practical exercises and meditation methods suggested in the chapter. Have you tried any of them? If so, how was your experience? If not, which ones do you want to investigate?

_____

_____

_____

_____

_____

_____

_____

Chapter Four: Unconditional Friendliness: The Spirit of Radical Acceptance

Key Lessons

The Power of Friendship: Tara Brach proposes the notion of "unconditional friendliness" as a vital component of radical acceptance. Being nice to yourself and others lays the groundwork for healing and change.

Replacing Self-Criticism with Friendliness: Many individuals have a tendency to criticize themselves, which leads to a cycle of pain. Brach teaches you how to recognize self-criticism and replace it with kinder, more compassionate inner dialogue.

The Role of Shame: Shame is examined as a widespread and damaging emotion that often underpins sentiments of unworthiness. You'll learn to recognize guilt and react to it with compassion and kindness.

Embracing Imperfection: Radical acceptance is letting go of the urge to be flawless and embracing your innate flaws. Brach invites you to find the beauty in your shortcomings and weaknesses.

Cultivating Self-Compassion: Self-compassion is a major subject in this chapter. Brach offers strategies for cultivating self-compassion, enabling you to treat yourself with the same care you would provide to a close friend.

The Inner Critic: The inner critic, a typical source of self-judgment, is investigated. You'll learn how to detach from its destructive messages and change your focus to self-encouragement.

Befriending Difficult Emotions: Unconditional friendliness extends to difficult emotions such as wrath, fear, and grief. Brach encourages you to approach these feelings with inquiry and compassion rather than resistance.

Healing Through Presence: The healing power of presence and attention is stressed. By being totally present with your inner experience, you may create a safe environment for healing and self-discovery.

Loving-Kindness Meditation: Loving-kindness meditation, a practice of providing goodwill to oneself and others, is offered as a transforming technique for fostering unconditional friendliness.

Integration into Daily Life: The chapter finishes with advice on how to incorporate the spirit of unconditional friendliness into your daily interactions and relationships, encouraging deeper understanding and connection.

Self Reflection Questions

In times of adversity or self-doubt, how do you usually connect to yourself? Are you self-critical or self-compassionate? Consider the effect of your self-talk.

_____

_____

_____

_____

_____

_____

_____

_____

Investigate any patterns of shame in your life.
When and how do you feel ashamed? How may
having a kind approach assist you in navigating
these situations?

_____

_____

_____

_____

_____

_____

_____

Consider one of your flaws or weaknesses. Can you
find the beauty or humanity in this element of
yourself? How may accepting flaws lead to better
self-acceptance?

_____

_____

_____

_____

_____

_____

_____

Consider your connection with your inner critic.
How does it affect your self-esteem and
decision-making? What methods can you use to
motivate yourself?

_____

_____

_____

_____

_____

_____

_____

_____

Have you ever tried loving-kindness meditation?
If so, how was your experience? If not, are you
prepared to investigate this practice as a means of
cultivating   more   self-compassion   and
friendliness?

_____

_____

_____

_____

_____

_____

_____

Chapter Five: Coming Home to Our Body: The Ground of Radical Acceptance

Key Lessons

Tara Brach highlights the intimate link between your mind and body. Being mindful of physiological sensations may assist you in accessing and processing deeply held emotions.

Embodiment Practices: The chapter covers several embodiment practices that anchor you in your body, such as body scans, mindful breathing, and yoga. These methods promote present-moment awareness.

Escaping the Prison of Overthinking: Brach investigates how the mind may get stuck in a loop of overthinking and rumination. Connecting with your body enables you to break free from this mental prison.

Healing Trauma: Physical tension and pain are common manifestations of traumatic events. Learning to be present with your physical feelings is an important step in healing trauma and releasing buried suffering.

Listening to Your Body's Insight: Your body has significant insight and intuition. You may make more connected and honest decisions by listening to physiological sensations and following your gut instincts.

Relaxation and Stress Reduction: Embodiment activities enhance relaxation and stress reduction. Brach provides ways for calming the nervous system and finding peace in the face of life's problems.

The Power of the Breath: Mindful breathing is presented as a simple but powerful strategy for anchoring your awareness in the present moment. You'll learn how to utilize your breath to relax your mind and body.

Accepting Physical suffering: Brach invites you to embrace physical suffering as a doorway to extreme acceptance. By addressing discomfort with presence, you may turn resistance into openness.

Body as Sanctuary: Your body may function as a sanctuary—a haven of shelter and tranquility. The chapter delves into how you might cultivate a feeling of safety and well-being inside your own body.

Bringing Mindfulness into Daily Life: Embodiment and mindfulness teachings are not restricted to formal meditation. Brach gives advice on how to incorporate these practices into your daily life for increased awareness and self-acceptance.

Self Reflection Questions

How frequently do you connect consciously with your body's sensations? Do you ever lose touch with your body? Consider the implications of this gap.

_____

_____

_____

_____

Have you ever been in a scenario when your body's senses supplied crucial knowledge or intuition? What did you learn from that event, and how did you respond?

_____

_____

_____

_____

_____

_____

_____

Examine your connection with overthinking and ruminating. How does overthinking affect your well-being? Can you think of a moment when grounding yourself in your body helped you interrupt the cycle of overthinking?

Consider any prior traumatic events or unresolved emotional anguish. Have you felt any bodily strain or pain as a result of these experiences? Consider the possible advantages of adopting embodiment techniques for recovery.

_____

_____

_____

_____

_____

_____

Experiment with a quick mindful breathing practice. How does concentrating on your breath affect your mental and physical state? Can you see yourself implementing this exercise into your regular routine?

_____

_____

_____

_____

_____

_____

_____

_____

Consider a recent incident in which you were physically uncomfortable or in pain. How did you deal with your discomfort? How may accepting it with awareness and acceptance result in a different experience?

_____

_____

_____

_____

_____

_____

_____

Chapter Six: Radical Acceptance of Desire: Awakening to the Source of Longing

Key Lessons

Understanding want: Tara Brach investigates the nature of want, highlighting that it is an essential component of being human. When motivated by yearning and attachment, desire may lead to pain.

The Cycle of Craving: This chapter digs into the cycle of craving and how we often seek external sources of pleasure to feed our cravings. Brach emphasizes how fleeting and unsatisfactory this striving is.

Recognizing the Source of Longing: Longing develops from a deep and sometimes unconscious feeling of separation or incompleteness. Brach pushes you to go into the underlying reasons for your yearning.

The Role of Mindfulness: Mindfulness is portrayed as a valuable technique for monitoring desire without an immediate response. You may increase your self-awareness by attention to your wants thoughtfully.

Instead of repressing or rejecting desire, Brach proposes a road to freedom via acceptance. You may have a more balanced and peaceful relationship with your wants if you acknowledge and understand them.

Reconnecting with completeness: Longing typically arises from a sense of separation from your inner completeness. Brach leads you through routines that will help you reconnect with your natural fullness.

The Gift of Gratitude: Gratitude is offered as an antidote to the unquenchable tendency of want. Cultivating thankfulness for what you currently have might help you change your emphasis from scarcity to abundance.

The notion of the hedonic treadmill is examined, demonstrating how individuals tend to adapt fast to favorable changes. Brach offers mindfulness as a means to get off the treadmill and enjoy life more completely.

Partnerships and Desire: Desire is important in partnerships. Brach explores how recognizing your own wants as well as those of others may lead to happier, more rewarding relationships.

The Path to genuine satisfaction: The chapter concludes with the concept that genuine satisfaction is discovered not in the exterior world but inside your own heart. Radical acceptance of desire may lead to a greater feeling of joy and calm.

Self Reflection Questions

Examine your connection with desire. What are some of your deepest desires? How have these desires affected your choices and actions?

_____

_____

_____

_____

_____

_____

_____

Investigate the idea of desire. Can you recall times when you pursued something with a strong desire only to discover fleeting gratification or even disappointment? What did you take away from these experiences?

_____

_____

_____

_____

_____

_____

How do you normally react to desire? Do you behave impulsively to meet impulses, or can you watch them attentively without taking immediate action? Consider the ramifications of your answers.

_____

_____

_____

_____

_____

_____

_____

_____

Consider times when you felt complete and satisfied. What events or behaviors resulted in these sentiments of fulfillment? How can you develop more of these experiences?

_____

_____

_____

_____

_____

_____

_____

_____

Investigate the importance of thankfulness in your life. Do you ever practice appreciation on purpose? How can expressing thankfulness affect your view on wishes and wants?

_____

_____

_____

_____

_____

_____

_____

Chapter Seven: Opening Our Hearts in the Face of Fear

Key Lessons

Understanding Fear: Tara Brach investigates the nature of fear, stressing that it is a common human experience. Fear may emerge in a variety of ways, ranging from anxiety and concern to deep-seated phobias.

Fear's Influence: Brach examines how fear may limit and influence our lives. It may result in avoidance habits, isolation, and a feeling of helplessness.

Recognizing Fear Patterns: This chapter urges you to become aware of your particular fear patterns. By recognizing reoccurring anxieties and their causes, you get insight into your emotional environment.

The Power of Mindfulness: Mindfulness is promoted as a transforming discipline for dealing with fear. By practicing mindfulness, you may perceive fear with greater clarity and non-reactivity.

Brach proposes the notion of radical acceptance as a means to embrace fear without judgment. Instead of opposing or denying fear, give it warmth and empathy.

Fear is seen as a source of insight and a messenger of unfulfilled needs. Brach trains you in listening to the signals that fear conveys and reacting with compassion.

Compassion is vital while coping with fear. Brach investigates how self-compassion might offset the self-criticism that commonly accompanies anxiety.

Bravery and Vulnerability: Facing fear takes bravery and a willingness to be vulnerable. Brach explores the interdependence of bravery and vulnerability in the process of opening your heart.

The Dread of Fear: Many people feel an additional layer of dread—the fear of fear itself. This dread of fear may amplify anxiety and impede your capacity to tackle underlying anxieties.

Transforming Fear into Freedom: The chapter concludes with the concept that by accepting fear with extreme acceptance and compassion, you may change it into a source of inner freedom and strength.

Self Reflection Questions:

Examine your connection with fear. What are some reoccurring concerns or anxieties in your life? How have your fears affected your decisions and actions?

_____

_____

_____

_____

_____

_____

_____

_____

Consider the influence of fear on your life. Are there any particular places where fear has held you back or hindered your potential? How has fear influenced your relationships and overall well-being?

_____

_____

_____

_____

_____

_____

_____

Investigate your own fear tendencies. Can you recognize fear triggers or situations? What physical and emotional feelings do you get when you are afraid?

_____

_____

_____

_____

_____

_____

_____

_____

Think about your mindfulness practice. How do you now address fear in your mindfulness practice, if at all? Is it possible to hone your capacity to notice fear without passing judgment?

_____

_____

_____

_____

_____

_____

_____

_____

Consider times when you have fought or rejected fear. What were the repercussions of this defiance? How may extreme acceptance of fear have resulted in a different outcome?

_____

_____

_____

_____

_____

_____

_____

Consider the signals in your fear. What may your fear be attempting to tell you about your needs, beliefs, or boundaries? How can you listen to these messages with more compassion?

_____

_____

_____

_____

_____

_____

Consider your ability to be compassionate to yourself. When you're afraid, how do you usually treat yourself? Are there ways you can cultivate greater self-compassion in moments of fear?

_____

_____

_____

_____

_____

_____

_____

Chapter Eight: Awakening Compassion for Ourselves: Becoming the Holder and the Held

Key Lessons

The Importance of Self-Compassion: Tara Brach highlights the need for self-compassion in the path of radical acceptance. Self-compassion entails treating oneself with the same love and care that you would provide to a close friend.

Self-Criticism and Its Impact: Brach investigates the harmful nature of self-criticism and how it relates to emotions of unworthiness and inadequacy. She emphasizes how self-judgment may be an obstacle to self-acceptance.

Recognizing Your Inner Critic: This chapter will help you discover your inner critic—the voice of self-judgment and self-doubt. Recognizing this essential inner conversation is the first step toward change.

The Role of Shame: Brach considers shame as a strong energy that promotes self-criticism and precludes self-compassion. Shame is often triggered by a feeling of failing to meet external or internal norms.

Shame Resilience: Building on the work of Brené Brown, Brach presents the notion of shame resilience—the capacity to identify and react to shame with self-compassion. Developing shame resistance is critical for self-acceptance.

The Power of Forgiveness: Forgiveness, both of ourselves and others, is investigated as a means of healing. Forgiveness does not condone destructive deeds but rather frees oneself from the grasp of bitterness and self-blame.

Self-Kindness activities: Brach provides activities and meditations to build self-kindness. These methods include providing oneself with calming words and caring gestures.

Meeting Your Vulnerable Self: This chapter will help you meet your vulnerable and wounded self with compassion. This entails admitting previous trauma and bringing comfort to your inner child.

Self-Compassion and Relationships: Brach investigates how self-compassion affects your capacity to participate in healthy relationships. When you carry yourself with compassion, you may be more real in your interactions with others.

Transforming Self-Criticism: The final lesson is that by practicing self-compassion, you may change self-criticism into self-acceptance and self-love. This change enables you to be both the holder and the held, providing caring care to oneself.

Self Reflection Questions

Consider your connection with self-compassion. How do you normally handle yourself when you make errors or experience difficulties? Do you prefer self-criticism or self-compassion?

_____

_____

_____

_____

_____

_____

_____

_____

Consider the influence of self-criticism on your well-being. How has self-judgment influenced your self-esteem and general happiness? Are there any particular situations when self-criticism has held you back?

_____

_____

_____

_____

_____

_____

_____

Examine your inner critic. Can you identify recurrent ideas or attitudes that lead to self-criticism? How does your inner critic reveal itself in your self-talk?

_____

_____

_____

_____

_____

_____

_____

Consider shame. Have you ever felt ashamed or unworthy in your life? How has shame changed your self-perception and behavior?

_____

_____

_____

Consider the concept of shame resiliency. Are there any tactics or practices you presently employ to react to shame with resilience and self-compassion? How can you improve your capacity to manage shame?

Chapter Nine: The RAIN of Compassion: An Applied Meditation for Healing and Freedom

Key Lessons

Tara Brach explains the RAIN meditation practice as a powerful tool for promoting compassion and healing. RAIN stands for Recognize, Allow, Investigate, and Nurture.

notice Your Experience: The first stage in the RAIN technique is to notice and acknowledge your present emotional state or experience. This entails stopping and being aware of your feelings without judgment.

Allowing Without Resistance: The "A" in RAIN indicates allowing your experience to be exactly as it is, without attempting to modify it or push it away. It's about permitting yourself to feel what you feel.

Curiosity: In the "I" stage, you dive deeper into your emotions with an inquisitive and non-judgmental attitude. You investigate the feelings, ideas, and beliefs related to your emotions.

Nurture with Compassion: The third phase, "Nurture," is reacting to your experience with self-compassion and care. You treat yourself with the same compassion and understanding that you would provide to a friend in suffering.

RAIN cultivates attentive awareness, allowing you to be more present with your emotions and ideas. This presence enables healing and change.

RAIN helps you to let go of your aversion to uncomfortable emotions. Acceptance and nonjudgmental awareness, on the other hand, may lead to healing.

Embracing Imperfection: RAIN encourages you to embrace your flaws and weaknesses, knowing that they are a natural part of being human.

Breaking the Cycle of Reactive Patterns: Using RAIN, you may break away from reactive patterns of behavior and cognition. This practice enables you to react to life's situations with more insight and compassion.

RAIN is not restricted to formal meditation; it can be incorporated into your everyday life. When dealing with stress, tough emotions, or interpersonal difficulties, you may use RAIN in real-time.

Self Reflection Questions

Have you ever tried RAIN meditation? If so, how was your experience? If not, how willing are you to attempt this technique for emotional healing and freedom?

_____

_____

_____

_____

_____

_____

_____

Think about a recent emotional event. Can you recall the precise feelings you had at the time? How did you usually react to such emotions?

_____

_____

_____

_____

_____

_____

_____

_____

Consider the concept of accepting without opposition. When confronted with unpleasant or disturbing feelings, how do you generally react? Do you prefer to oppose or repress them, or can you allow them to be present?

_____

_____

_____

_____

_____

_____

_____

_____

Investigate the notion of inquiry with curiosity. Consider approaching a recent emotional event with inquiry and nonjudgment. What insights or discoveries may you make concerning the nature of your emotions?

_____

_____

_____

_____

_____

_____

Consider the concept of compassionate caring. When you're going through a difficult emotional situation, how do you usually treat yourself? Can you imagine treating yourself with the same attention and tenderness you would treat a friend?

_____

_____

_____

_____

_____

_____

_____

_____

Consider the function of attentive awareness in the RAIN practice. How may being more attentive and present with your emotions enhance your general well-being?

_____

_____

_____

_____

_____

_____

_____

Consider using RAIN in your everyday life. Can you imagine applying the RAIN approach in real time when confronted with challenging circumstances or interactions? How may it alter your approach to problems and conflicts?

_____

_____

_____

_____

_____

_____

_____

Chapter Ten: Widening the Circles of Compassion: The Bodhisattva's Path

Key Lessons

The Bodhisattva Ideal: Tara Brach explains the Bodhisattva ideal, a major notion in Mahayana Buddhism. Bodhisattvas are those dedicated to relieving the suffering of all creatures and assisting them in attaining enlightenment.

Compassion as a Way of Life: The Bodhisattva's path is founded on compassion. It entails making compassion a way of life and actively seeking to alleviate suffering, both in oneself and in others.

The Inner and Outward Journeys: A Bodhisattva's path comprises both inner change and outward service. It is about cultivating knowledge and compassion inside oneself and then spreading that compassion to the rest of the world.

Compassionate Circles Extend: The Bodhisattva path begins with self-compassion and widens to encompass loved ones, acquaintances, strangers, and even perceived adversaries. It encourages you to tear through the walls that divide you from others.

Recognizing Our Oneness: The path of the Bodhisattva is founded on the realization of all creatures' oneness. It acknowledges that your well-being is inextricably tied to the well-being of others.

Loving-kindness Practice: The development of loving-kindness (Metta) is an important practice for Bodhisattvas. It entails cultivating sentiments of love, compassion, and kindness toward oneself and all creatures.

Freedom from the Prison of Self: By actively practicing compassion and loving-kindness, you may liberate yourself from the prison of self-obsession and ego-centered worries. This release leads to more inner serenity and contentment.

Mending the planet: The Bodhisattva's path is for more than simply personal salvation; it is about mending the planet. It entails taking action to solve social and environmental challenges, as well as striving for justice and equality.

bravery and Resilience: Walking the Bodhisattva path requires bravery and resilience. It entails confronting the world's suffering with an open heart and a determination to make a difference.

Tara Brach delves into the Bodhisattva vow, a formal commitment to the Bodhisattva path. Taking this promise represents a strong commitment to the well-being of all creatures.

Self Reflection Questions:

Consider your knowledge of the Bodhisattva ideal. How does the concept of actively seeking to relieve the suffering of all creatures strike you? What obstacles or worries does it bring for you?

_____

_____

_____

_____

_____

_____

_____

_____

Consider kindness as a way of life. How would your life change if you made compassion a primary driving principle? What adjustments would you need to make in your everyday behaviors and attitudes?

_____

_____

_____

_____

_____

_____

_____

Investigate the notion of the Bodhisattva's inner and outside journey. How do you now combine your inner development and self-care with your involvement in helping others and creating a good influence on the world?

_____

_____

_____

_____

_____

_____

_____

Consider the practice of broadening circles of compassion. Is it difficult for you to feel compassion for some persons or groups of people? What obstacles prohibit you from offering compassion to them?

_____

_____

_____

_____

_____

_____

_____

_____

Consider the interdependence of all creatures. How does this realization affect your feeling of duty to people and the planet? In what ways do you now demonstrate this connectivity in your life?

_____

_____

_____

_____

_____

_____

_____

_____

Consider the practice of loving-kindness. Have you ever tried loving-kindness meditation or a similar practice? How may practicing loving-kindness toward yourself and others enhance your well-being?

_____

_____

_____

_____

_____

_____

_____

Chapter Eleven: Recognizing Our Basic Goodness: The Gateway to a Forgiving and Loving Heart

Key Lessons

Tara Brach proposes the notion of "basic goodness," which is the intrinsic, unconditioned, and pure character of all beings. Recognizing this essential goodness is a critical first step toward self-acceptance and compassion.

Healing Through Self-Forgiveness: Self-forgiveness is a critical component of accepting fundamental goodness. It entails letting go of self-blame and self-judgment and accepting that you are worthy of love and forgiveness.

The Power of Self-Compassion: Self-compassion is a means to nourish and cherish your inherent goodness. It entails treating oneself with the same love and understanding that you would provide to a close friend.

Shame is a highly unpleasant and lonely feeling. Recognizing your underlying goodness allows you to transcend shame into self-acceptance and self-compassion.

Embracing your core goodness helps you to open to vulnerability without fear. You recognize that being vulnerable is not a sign of weakness, but rather a reflection of your true nature.

Forgiving Others: Just as you can forgive yourself, you can also forgive others. Forgiveness is a powerful act for releasing bitterness and rebuilding broken relationships.

The Healing Power of Love: Love is a transforming force that can heal and restore even the most damaged portions of yourself and your relationships. Recognizing your inherent goodness helps you to access this healing force.

Living From the Heart: As you acknowledge your inherent goodness and practice self-forgiveness and self-compassion, you will be able to live more from the heart. This entails making decisions and acting based on love and compassion.

Deepening Relationships: Embracing fundamental goodness improves your capacity to connect with people truthfully and generously. It lays the groundwork for deeper, more lasting partnerships.

Recognizing fundamental goodness is a continuous activity, not a one-time discovery. To keep the awareness alive, everyday mindfulness and self-compassion are required.

Self Reflection Questions

Consider the notion of fundamental goodness. Do you think that every creature has an inherent and unconditioned goodness? Why or why not? How would your life alter if you completely adopted this concept?

_____

_____

_____

_____

_____

_____

_____

_____

Examine the concept of self-forgiveness. Do you
struggle to forgive yourself for previous errors or
actions? What measures can you take to begin the
process of self-forgiveness?

_____

_____

_____

_____

_____

_____

_____

_____

Consider the practice of self-compassion. How do
you now handle yourself when you make a mistake
or confront a challenging situation? What would it

look like to react to yourself with more self-compassion?

_____

_____

_____

_____

_____

_____

_____

Consider the role that shame plays in your life. Are there any places where shame has kept you back or caused you pain? How could acknowledging your inherent goodness assist you in transforming shame into self-acceptance?

_____

_____

_____

_____

_____

_____

_____

_____

Consider the idea of vulnerability. Do you shun vulnerability or embrace it as a source of authenticity? How may acknowledging your inherent goodness alter your relationship with vulnerability?

_____

_____

_____

_____

_____

_____

_____

Investigate the concept of forgiveness, both for yourself and others. Is there anyone you need to forgive or ask forgiveness from? What measures can you take to begin the process of forgiveness?

Consider the healing power of love. How has love helped you heal your own scars or repair relationships? How can you incorporate more love into your everyday life and relationships with others?

Chapter Twelve: Awakening Together: Practicing Radical Acceptance in Relationship

Key Lessons

Relationships as Mirrors: Relationships act as mirrors, reflecting back our own habits, scars, and unsolved problems. Adopting radical acceptance in relationships starts with self-awareness.

The Dance of Blame and Defense: It's usual in partnerships to participate in a dance of blame and defense. Recognizing this pattern and accepting responsibility for your role in it is critical for healing and progress.

Deep listening is a basic ability for practicing radical acceptance in partnerships. It entails being totally present and attentive to the other person's point of view, even if it varies from your own.

Embracing Vulnerability: Vulnerability is an important aspect of close partnerships. Sharing your whole self, including your anxieties and vulnerabilities, creates connection and trust.

Radical Acceptance involves radical honesty—being honest with yourself and others about your ideas, emotions, and needs. It requires both bravery and vulnerability.

Compassion for Differences: Embracing differences in a relationship involves acknowledging each person's unique viewpoint and needs without attempting to alter or control them.

Forgiveness in partnerships: Forgiveness is a continual process in partnerships. It entails letting go of resentments and choosing to concentrate on healing and progress.

Intimacy and Connection: Radical acceptance in relationships leads to greater intimacy and connection. It enables you to be fully seen and accepted by your spouse, and vice versa.

Resolving Conflict Mindfully: Mindful conflict resolution entails addressing differences with openness, compassion, and a commitment to finding mutually beneficial solutions.

Awakening Together: Practicing radical acceptance in a partnership is a shared path of awakening. It entails helping one another become more mindful and loving humans.

Self Reflection Questions

Consider your present or previous relationships. Is there a pattern of blame and defense? What role have you played in these patterns, and how can you accept responsibility for your part?

Consider the significance of thorough listening in your interactions. Do you listen actively and intently, or do you find yourself interrupting or preparing your answer as the other person speaks?

Investigate the topic of vulnerability in your interactions. Are there any situations where you find it difficult to be vulnerable, or where you are afraid of being judged or rejected for your actual self?

Consider extreme honesty in your dealings with people. Do you ever suppress your genuine thoughts or feelings? How may practicing radical honesty improve your relationships?

Consider accepting diversity in your relationships. Do you strive to modify or control the people you care about, or can you fully accept and recognize their distinct opinions and needs?

Consider forgiveness to be a continual activity in your relationships. Are there any resentments or issues that you need to confront and resolve? How can forgiveness help with healing and growth?

Investigate the concept of intimacy and connection. In which relationships do you feel most noticed, welcomed, and connected? What variables contribute to this sensation of intimacy?

Chapter Thirteen: Recognizing Our True Nature

Key Takeaways
actual Nature: Realizing our actual nature is the climax of the path of radical acceptance. It entails realizing the timeless and unconditioned nature of our existence.

Beyond Ego: Our actual essence lives beyond the boundaries of the egoic self. It is a wellspring of knowledge, love, and clarity that is always available when we let go of ego-driven attachments and identifications.

The Illusion of Separation: The belief in separation is a primary cause of pain. Realizing our actual essence entails overcoming the illusion of separation and embracing our oneness with all of existence.

Awakening to Presence: Presence is the doorway to recognizing our genuine essence. Being totally present in each moment helps us to access the depth and wisdom of our real selves.

Living from Essence: Living from our actual essence is making decisions and living in accordance with our innermost values and knowledge. It is a way of aware and compassionate life.

Compassion as a Natural Expression: When we know our actual essence, compassion becomes a natural and spontaneous expression of who we are. It is not something we must develop; it just happens.

Freedom from Suffering: Recognizing our actual nature frees us from the circle of suffering. We no longer cling to fleeting identifications and discover freedom in our unconditioned nature.

The Next Step in Practice: Recognizing our actual nature is not the conclusion of the path, but rather a fresh beginning. It is a continuous practice of increasing our connection to our true selves.

Service and Contribution: Living from our actual nature leads to a natural desire to serve and contribute to the well-being of others and the planet. It is a method of showing our love and oneness.

The Joy of Being: Recognizing our actual nature provides us with a tremendous feeling of joy and contentment. It is the delight of being, rather than the chase of outward achievements.

Self Reflection Questions

Consider the idea of genuine nature. Do you think you have a timeless and unconditioned essence inside you? How may realizing this essence affect your life?

Consider the limits of the egoic self. Are there any attachments or identifications that you identify as ego-driven? How could getting rid of these attachments bring you closer to discovering your actual nature?

Examine the illusion of separation. In what ways do you feel separated from people or the environment around you? How can you build a stronger feeling of interconnectedness?

Consider the significance of presence in discovering your genuine nature. Are there times when you feel totally present and connected to your inner self? What techniques assist you in achieving this level of presence?

Consider living from the essence. How can you link your decisions and behaviors with your innermost values and wisdom? What changes may this alignment bring to your life?

Consider compassion as a natural reflection of your genuine character. How do spontaneous gestures of compassion and kindness feel? How can you support this natural expression?

Consider the notion of liberation from pain. Is there somewhere in your life where holding to ephemeral identifications or attachments causes you pain? How could realizing your actual nature offer you relief from your suffering?

Final Evaluation Questions

How has your knowledge of radical acceptance grown as you read the book, and how has it informed your view on self-compassion and self-worth?

Consider a particular instance or incident in your life when you utilized the principles of radical acceptance. How has this practice affected your emotional well-being and how you connect to yourself and others?

In what areas of your life do you find it most difficult to embrace radical acceptance? How may you focus on applying these ideas to those areas to promote personal development and healing?

Consider the notion of "Where does it hurt?" as a way of understanding and connecting with people on a deeper level. How can you use this question in your interactions with friends, family, and coworkers to create more sympathetic and compassionate relationships?

Investigate the notion of accepting vulnerability in your life. Are there any circumstances or relationships in which you tend to avoid vulnerability, and how may lean into vulnerability lead to deeper authenticity and connection?

Consider the importance of forgiveness in your life. Do you have any old grudges or resentments? How can you begin the process of forgiveness to relieve the load of these bad emotions?

Consider your personal relationships and the patterns of blame and defense that may emerge. How can you take deliberate measures to break away from these habits and promote more open and understanding communication with your loved ones?

Consider the lessons on discovering your actual self. What activities or experiences have brought you closer to a feeling of your actual self beyond ego?

Consider the function of presence in your everyday life. Is it difficult for you to be totally present in some situations? What tactics or mindfulness practices can you use to improve your capacity to be present in the moment?

Investigate the concept of living from your essence and making decisions that are in line with your innermost ideals. What particular activities or adjustments in your life can you commit to that reflect this alignment and lead to a more fulfilled and purpose-driven existence?

Consider compassion as a natural reflection of your genuine character. How can you build more compassion in your everyday thoughts and deeds, not just toward others but also toward yourself?

Consider your unique path of self-acceptance and self-love. How has reading Tara Brach's "Radical Acceptance" aided your personal road of healing and growth? What thoughts or practices will you take away from this book?

Made in the USA
Las Vegas, NV
10 December 2024

13766187R00056